Grief Journal Prompts

Remembering Your Loved One Through Journaling

Introduction

After I lost my dad I had found writing to be therapeutic for me as well as grief counseling. I found the best way for me to journal was through writing prompts. I began to create my own writing prompts to help me process my father's death. I had found there were things I didn't know about my father like what high school he graduated from. In some ways this may be a discovery journey for you. Some of these prompts may be too hard to do right now and that is okay. I haven't done all of the prompt yet, but I wrote them out because someday I would like to. It may even take years before you are able to finish every prompt and that is okay. The pain of grief can be abstract. I compiled these prompts as a way to help me remember my father and I hope they can help you remember your loved one too.

About Your Loved One

What is your loved ones name?

When is their birthday?

When did your loved one pass?

Day 1. Describe the first time you met your loved one or the first memory you have of them.

Day 2.What was their favorite season? Describe a memory of them in that season.

Day 3. What was their favorite hobby? What were their talents? Write about how they impacted you.

Day 4. What was their favorite holiday? Describe how they celebrated it?

Day 5. Write about your favorite memory with them.

Day 6. What song reminds you of your loved one?
Describe a memory with the song. How does
hearing the song affect you now?

Day 7. Where was your favorite place to go together?

Day 8. What do you miss most about them?

Day 9. Describe their facial features?

Day 10. Describe their personality.

Day 11. What random thing makes you think about your loved one? For some people it's a smell for other people it's an object like a pen or purse.

Day 12. Do you know what High School they went to? Did they get to graduate?

Day 13. What is their favorite bible verse or quote that inspired them.

Day 14. Is there a favorite clothing item of theirs that has sentimental meaning to you?

Day 15. Write them a letter of things you wish you had told them.

Day 16. Is there a symbolic way you have thought to keep their memory alive? (Some people keep a special candle or a type of flower in the house or yard).

Day 17. Are there any relationships that have changed since the death. Does that make you happy or sad? Write a letter to the people you have felt you lossed along with the death of your loved one. (The letter isn't meant to be given to them).

Day 18 Have you felt people have understood how to support you during the grieving process or do you feel they want you to rush through the grieving process and pretend you are okay?

Day 19. Describe your favorite place to go together?

Day 20. What do you wish could have been different in the relationship? Maybe you had a parent who died who seldom called you and you wish they were less distant. Maybe a sibling died and you guys had lost touch. Maybe you had nothing in common with the loved one who died and you wish you did.

Day 21. What dreams are left unfulfilled because of the death? If a spouse died you may have lost the dream of retiring together or starting a business together. If a parent died you may have lost the dream of having them walk you down the aisle on your wedding day.

Day 22. Describe how you feel on their birthday.

Day 21. What was the best birthday gift they ever gave you?
What was the best birthday gift you ever gave them?

Day 22. What was the best Christmas gift you ever gave them?
What was the best Christmas gift they ever gave you?

Day 23. Did they like to cook? What was their favorite meal? Did you ever cook for them?

Day 24. What movie makes you think of them?

Day 25. Is there anything you would like them to know you forgive them for? Write them a letter of forgiveness.

Day 26. Is there anything you need them to forgive you for? Write them a letter asking them for forgiveness.

Day 27. What kind of parent, spouse, sibling, friend, significant other, grandparent, were they?

Day 28. Did they like to read? What was their favorite book?

Day 29. Did they like art? What was their favorite painting?

Day 30. Do any colors make you think of your loved one?

Day 31. Describe a place you use to always go together. Some people say church is harder to go to because that person isn't there anymore. Maybe you always had coffee together in the morning at your favorite coffee shop. Saturday mornings you always went to the thrift shops together and they aren't there anymore. You may have always played Bingo on Wednesday nights and now it's not the same. Write about how that loss has affected you.

Day 32. Did your loved one like cold weather or hot weather?

Day 33.What was their favorite song?

Day 34. Did your loved one like snow? Describe your favorite winter memory.

Day 35. Did your loved one like the hot weather and the beach? Describe your favorite summer memory with them.

Day 36. Did your loved one like flowers? What was their favorite flower?

Day 37. Describe the house they lived in? What type of car did they drive?

Day 38. Did your loved one like sports? What was their favorite sports team?
What was your favorite sports memory with them.

Day 39. Did you take walks together? Describe where you walked. It may even be walks around the nursing home or hospital halls.

Day 40. Was their nursing staff you and your loved one grew really close to? Write a letter thanking them for their care. You can send it if you feel comfortable.

Day 41. Are you relieved by your loved one's death at all? (Sometimes people are relieved because the person is out of pain and they are not sick anymore. Sometimes the burden of being a caretaker is too much, especially if you are an older couple or have a lot of other demands).

Day 42. Not all relationships are easy write about the things that made this relationship hard. It could be an addiction they had. You may have been the caretaker and they may have seemed needy at times. You may have had to sacrifice some things to be there for them.

Day 43. Did they have a pet? Write about their pet. You may have liked the pet or you may have not liked the pet. You may have been allergic to the pet.

Day 44. What state was your loved one born in? Is there anywhere else they would have rather lived?

Day 45. Did you ever go on vacation together or a weekend trip? Describe it. Is there any place you wish you could have gone together?

Day 46. Describe the funeral. Did you get to plan it? Was there anything you wish would have been different? Was there any family tension?

Day 47. Can you picture the person in heaven? Write about how you see them in heaven. Write about how you envision your first encounter with them in heaven.

Day 48. Take the letters of their first name and write characteristics about them. Example: Tim: Talented, Intelligent, Makes people feel special.

Day 49. Is there anything special you would like to do on the day of their death anniversary? It could be writing them a letter or volunteering at an organization they liked. You could invite people over to have a day of remembrance.

Day 50. Do you know their favorite hot beverage?

Day 51. Besides the main lose of losing a parent, friend, sibling, child, spouse, grandparent, niece, nephew what are the other loses you have experienced? It may be the loss of a walking partner. The loss of the person who drove or was in charge of finances. The loss of a tennis partner.

Day 52. What day of the week was their favorite? Was there a certain day that was special between you?

Day 53. What was their political affiliation? Did you agree or disagree?

Day 54. Was there a candy that was special to them?

Day 55. Write a letter thanking the person for the time they had in your life.

Made in the USA
San Bernardino, CA
08 April 2019